D1398296

BIG DATA

KRISTIN FONTICHIARO

Published in the United States of America by Cherry Lake Publishing
Ann Arbor, Michigan
www.cherrylakepublishing.com

Series Adviser: Kristin Fontichiaro
Photo Credits: Cover and page 1, ©Mark Agnor/Shutterstock; page 5, ©Oleksii Shalamov/Shutterstock; page 6, ©Brian A Jackson/Shutterstock; page 8, ©bikeriderlondon/Shutterstock; page 11, ©Icatnews/Shutterstock; page 12, ©iofoto/Shutterstock; page 14, ©THPStock/Shutterstock; page 17, ©Richard Paul Kane/Shutterstock; page 18, ©AF archive/Alamy Stock Photo; page 20, ©Uber Images/Shutterstock; page 22, ©TaLaNoVa/Shutterstock; page 25, ©Monkey Business Images/Shutterstock; page 26, ©Vanatchanan/Shutterstock; page 28, ©K Woodgyer/Shutterstock; page 29, ©Festa/Shutterstock

Library of Congress Cataloging-in-Publication Data has been filed and is available at catalog.loc.gov

Cherry Lake Publishing would like to acknowledge the work of the Partnership for
21st Century Learning. Please visit *www.p21.org* for more information.

Printed in the United States of America
Corporate Graphics

ABOUT THE AUTHOR

Kristin Fontichiaro teaches and studies how we learn about data at the University of Michigan School of Information.

TABLE OF CONTENTS

CHAPTER 1

Big Data Is Everywhere

Do you have a special card you show each time you shop at a certain store? A loyalty card or shopping card? If you do, then you are part of the Big Data revolution. You may think that by swiping your loyalty or shopping card, you're just getting discounts. But behind the scenes, a whole bunch of information about you is being stored.

This collection of information is so big that it wouldn't fit on most regular computers. When there is that much information involved, we call it Big Data.

You may have heard about Big Data in the news, but what is it? Well, you already know what *big* means. *Data* is another word for information in the form of numbers or words.

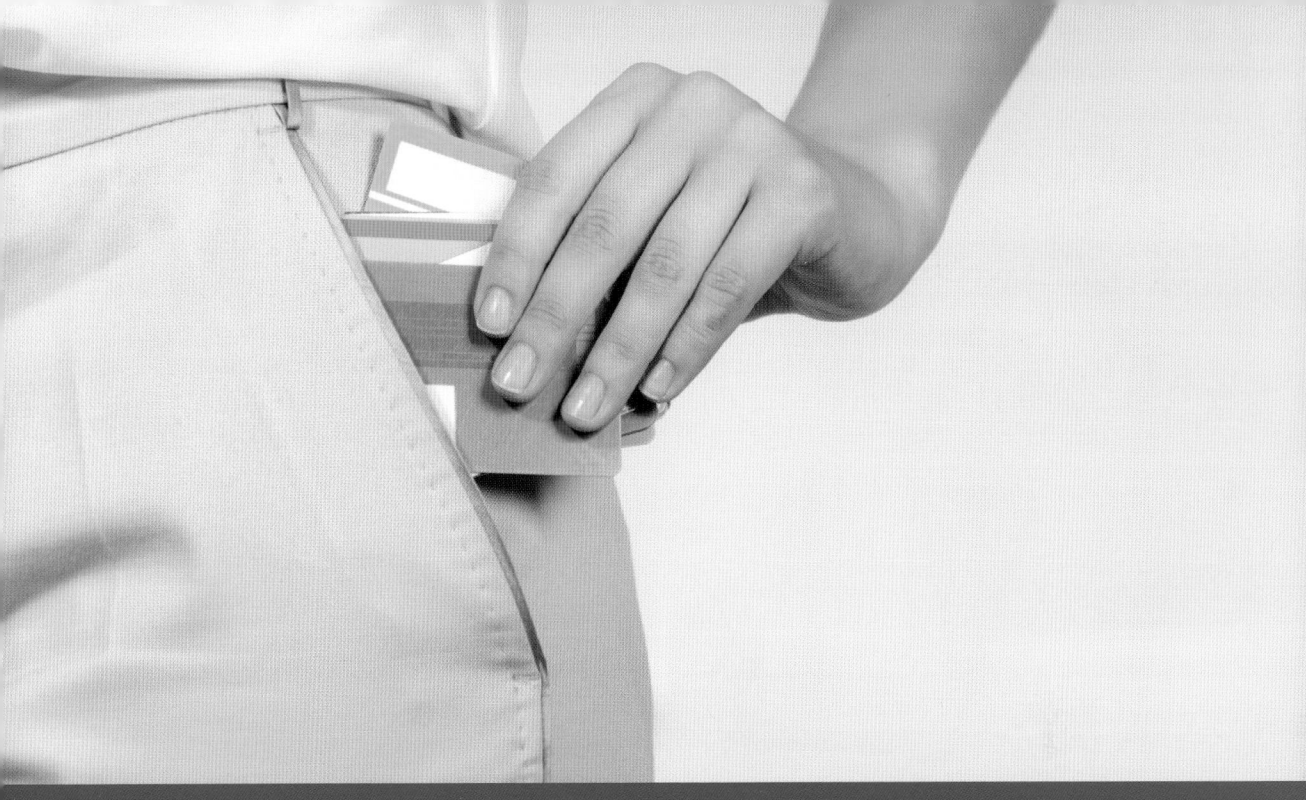
Your family might have a whole pile of different cards for different stores. Each one tracks information about you.

Let's say a woman named Jane swipes her loyalty store card at the grocery store. When the card is swiped, it tells the computer running the cash register to unlock special sale prices for some items. Hooray for Jane! However, the card can also collect a lot of other stuff that helps the business. From that one swipe, the computer system knows Jane's name, address, and other personal information. It can then keep track of everything she buys.

Wait. How does the system know so much about this shopper? It's simple. Back when Jane first got her card, she was asked to fill out a form with her name, address, and other personal

Giving up some personal information is a requirement for many deals and promotions at stores and other businesses.

information. Everything she wrote down was entered into the system. Each piece of information is one more data point in the computer system. Over time, this data adds up.

Big Data isn't a place or a company or an organization. It's the idea that it's now possible, with the help of technology, to gather up tiny bits of information almost at the speed of light, often without people realizing it's happening. Big Data doesn't just appear. It is assembled over time. As you learned earlier, a single swipe of a grocery store shopping card has the power to send data in a lot of different directions. Anytime there is a digital device that can capture movements, keystrokes, mouse clicks, or even

Rule of Thumb

When you are offered something for free by a company, ask yourself, "What am I giving in order to receive this bonus? Am I okay with that?" You might be willing to give up the information in exchange for a good deal, but you also might not!

Every time you swipe a card at a store, you are contributing to Big Data.

sounds, it becomes possible for computers and other machines to collect data much faster than it could ever be collected by humans.

But Big Data isn't just a jumbled collection of information. Complex computer programs use math formulas known as **algorithms** to sort out the information, find patterns, and make decisions.

But where does Big Data come from?

Try This

*Ask a trusted adult if you can sit together and look through the cards in his or her wallet. Which cards might send data to a big **server** somewhere online when they are used?*

For example, a bank may keep an eye out for unusual purchases on a credit card. Its computer systems scan incoming charges for something that seems out of place, such as a store not usually visited, an area of the world where the customer has not shopped recently, or even an unusually large purchase.

Ask the adult which store or loyalty cards they use. What benefits come from those cards? What data is given away in exchange? What information are you and the adult okay with sharing? What kind of information would make you nervous to share?

CHAPTER 2

Where Does Big Data Come From?

Let's go back to the grocery line. As Jane puts items on the counter to check out, the cashier scans each one. As he does, the computer system is learning:

- *The kinds of food that Jane likes to buy.* The system might decide to match up her purchases with coupons for related products. It might also notice patterns among shoppers who have things in common. For example, maybe women prefer to buy Diet Coke, while men prefer Coke Zero. That information could be sold later to the Coca-Cola Company, which could use that information to adjust the way it advertises its products.

- *Which items Jane buys at the same time.* It might realize that she often buys cheese and crackers together. If the computer

Coupons are a common reward for customers who use loyalty cards at stores.

notices the same pattern with other shoppers, it might signal to the store manager that placing crackers next to the cheese might help sell more products.

- *How much Jane spent that day.* If Jane spends a lot of money each time she shops, the system might flag her as a VIP customer. Next time she visits and swipes her card, perhaps the computer will notify the cashier of her special status and offer her a bonus item, such as a cloth shopping bag instead of paper. At a restaurant, swiping your loyalty card might get you free chips and salsa.

Big Data allows companies to track which products are popular among men, women, or other categories of people.

- *How often Jane shops.* Does she usually come in every week but hasn't been there in six months? Maybe the system is set up to page the manager to come to the checkout lane to thank the customer for returning.
- *How many of each product the store still has in stock.* This is known as keeping **inventory**. Workers don't have to count items on the shelves because the computer is doing it with each checkout.
- *Where Jane lives.* Maybe the grocery store is thinking of building a new store. By keeping track of shoppers' zip codes, they can get a clearer picture of where they should build it. By learning the kinds of products people buy in different zip codes, companies can also build **personas** about the kinds of people who live in a certain area.

Whew! That is a lot of data! Some of these features, like getting a free cloth bag or a hello from the manager, might be really appealing to a shopper. Others, like keeping inventory and knowing the patterns of what people buy, are more of a help to the grocery store. And some of the data is best used by companies or government agencies that aren't in the store at all.

ack
2.00 ea
/P
$1.50 ea
n Special
@ $4.99/
Special
@ $1.00 ea

Description

Jap Pumpkin
qty 2.1156 @ $1.99 ea
Potato Unwashed
1.330 kg @ $2.49/kg
Onion Brown P/P
Ca   qty 1 @ $1.50 ea
       Apples Special
       0.845 kg @ $1.99/kg
Rou Garlic
       0.085 kg @ $14.99/kg
       avocado Small
       qty 1 @ $0.99 ea
       Apricots
       0.430 kg @ $4.99/kg
       Lettuce Plain
       qty 1 @ $0.99 ea
       Cucumber Contin

hanas Large
.625 kg @ $3.49/kg
pples Special
    kg @ $1.99/kg

$1.50

Am

14

Onio
qty 1 @ $2.

Anytime you post things to social media, buy something with a credit card, take a state standardized test, or fill out an online poll, you're contributing tiny bits of data and information to huge servers. Along the way, you're having fun with your friends, buying what you need, making it through school, or finding out which Harry Potter character is most like you. We're always going to be trading some data for some service. But the big question is, did you know that all of this information was being collected?

What's a Persona?

A persona is not a real person. It's a made-up "character" that businesspeople use to represent a type of person. It's a **composite**: a collection of a lot of habits and traits that a larger group of people possesses. Personas are created as a shortcut for talking about the kinds of people who live in a certain area, use a certain product, have certain hobbies, and more. Sometimes, these personas are called "market segmentations."

Businesses, marketers, and the local government can look at personas to think about how to provide better services. Is the population growing? If so, is it time to build a new drugstore? A hospital? A school? A highway?

CHAPTER 3

Big Data = Data + Algorithm

Sometimes, collecting a lot of data in one place makes it possible to get insights that have never before been possible. The 2011 movie *Moneyball* is based on the true story of the Oakland A's Major League Baseball team. The team did not have a big enough budget to hire a bunch of star players. However, a data **analyst** started organizing player data in new and unique ways. This helped him uncover hidden trends among lesser-known players. These players weren't big stars, but they had the specific skills the team needed to win games. Better data meant a better team!

Imagine you're interested in starting a fantasy baseball team. There's a cool new Web site that helps you staff your dream team by analyzing both a player's stats and also fan opinions of the player. That seems to make sense. It's combining known baseball

A huge amount of data is collected about the performance of professional athletes.

In *Moneyball*, actor Jonah Hill played a character based on real-life data analyst Paul DePodesta, who has used data to help manage several professional sports teams.

stats with what fans know. That's more information, right? So why is it that your team isn't performing the way you anticipated? One day, you realize you left the site open on your computer. Your little brother was there, clicking over and over on the worst player's icon. Oh no! He's accidentally adding bad data to the site. The site didn't know that he was a toddler, and not a real baseball fan, racking up inaccurate points.

That's the challenge of Big Data. We rarely know exactly who has submitted data and what the secret formula, or algorithm, was for calculating it. Taking data crunching away from humans gives us faster information, but the processes of Big Data analysis are still new. We're not yet able to be sure that it's better information.

Think back to the fantasy baseball site. Maybe your brother was partly to blame. But what else could be causing the weird results that you cannot see? Maybe there's something in the algorithm that you didn't know. Maybe someone set up the formula not to count bunts. Maybe rookies get more weight added to their stats. Or maybe the stats only get recalculated on Sundays, and so the data is outdated by Saturday. Maybe fans aren't very good at predicting success. Maybe the site is mainly designed to sell ad space, so its creators aren't really concerned about great data.

All of these are human decisions that affect the way the numbers look. And those numbers are what you're using to figure out what makes a great baseball player. Maybe the data gets

Rule of Thumb

Big Data has the potential for us to rapidly discover new and valuable patterns.

You might be confused at first if data doesn't work the way you expect it to.

skewed on purpose. More likely, the creators of the algorithm didn't think of everything or even just made a mistake!

So does that mean Big Data is cool or creepy? It depends. Let's look at another example. Many communities now use Big Data algorithms for something called predictive policing. At first, the idea sounds great: Find the parts of a community where the most crime happens, and then send a larger number of police officers to that area. That way, there should always be plenty of police where the crimes occur. Lots of towns and cities are using Big Data in this way.

But think about this idea some more. If there are more police in one neighborhood, more arrests will take place there. This

Try This

Imagine you were collecting mouse clicks in every computer lab in your school district. You would know exactly what each person was clicking on and when they were clicking on it. What do you think you could learn from those clicks? What kind of notice would you want to give to students, teachers, and staff in your school so they were aware that this information was being collected?

One small mistake can completely throw off the results of data analysis.

raises the crime rate in that area. And, with less police in other areas, guess what happens? Arrests happen less frequently in those areas, and the crime rate there goes down.

So with predictive policing, an unexpected problem occurs: "Safe areas" start to look safer than they really might be, and "dangerous" areas appear even more dangerous. Wait a minute. That isn't what the police were trying to do. This is a serious mistake because houses in "safer" areas are worth more than those in "dangerous" areas, because everybody wants to live in a place the police say is safer. People prefer to shop, eat, play, and go to school in areas they think are safer.

As you can see, Big Data is way more complicated than it seems. Even when it tries to be helpful, it can still mess up. In part, this is because Big Data is a pretty new idea.

Rule of Thumb

Big Data isn't necessarily good or evil.

CHAPTER 4

Citizen Science: Big Data for Good

What does a scientist look like? You might think of someone in a white lab coat spending years experimenting in a laboratory, working alone and hoping to have a "Eureka!" moment.

Today, scientists don't have to work by themselves to collect data in a lab or in nature. They can set up an experiment and ask volunteers to help them carry it out. Citizen science is a practice where experts and ordinary citizens work together to collect and sort through a lot of data in a much shorter amount of time.

Experts set up the systems to collect data. They outline how and what kinds of data should be collected. For example, a scientist at a major university near you may want to know how many oak trees are in your town. She might draw boxes on a map

Collecting data is a big part of a scientist's job.

to define specific spaces and then assign a volunteer to each box of land to count the trees. With enough volunteers, all the trees could be counted in a single day. That is a lot faster than if the scientist did all the work alone.

Some projects take far longer than days. For several years, the eBird.org project from Cornell University has gathered data collected by hundreds of passionate amateur bird-watchers. Find a bird? Catalog it for the system! So much information is collected by eBird each year that the federal government relies on it for annual reporting information.

Anyone can volunteer to join a citizen science project.

Zooniverse.org invites volunteers to analyze photographs and other data from nature. PenguinWatch is one of its best-known projects. It sets up cameras in remote regions to take photos to track penguin counts and locations. This means people can contribute data without leaving home or facing cold temperatures. By simply clicking on photos to identify where the penguins are, you can be one of hundreds of volunteers to help make enormous data collection possible for researchers.

Scistarter.com is another site that invites volunteers to track scientific data. Maybe you want to fill out a weekly survey about who around you has the flu. This helps experts get a better sense of where and when illness occurs around the country. Maybe you're interested in helping to track where packages go or in sharing air quality data you collect in your backyard.

Rule of Thumb

For citizen science to be an effective way of gathering large amounts of data, everyone has to agree on what to count, when to count it, and where to put the data.

Do you like watching birds? Visit *http://feederwatch.org* and sign up to contribute data from your bird feeder!

Proteins are important substances in the human body. The more scientists know about how they work, the better they will understand how to keep people healthy. Proteins tend to bunch up or "fold" inside the body. From the ways the folds happen, scientists can figure out what the proteins are doing. Observing this used to be an extremely time-consuming process. But thanks to citizen science volunteers, what once took years can now take just days. Fold.it is a site that invites volunteers to play puzzle games. In doing so, they help scientists visualize all the possible ways in which proteins can fold.

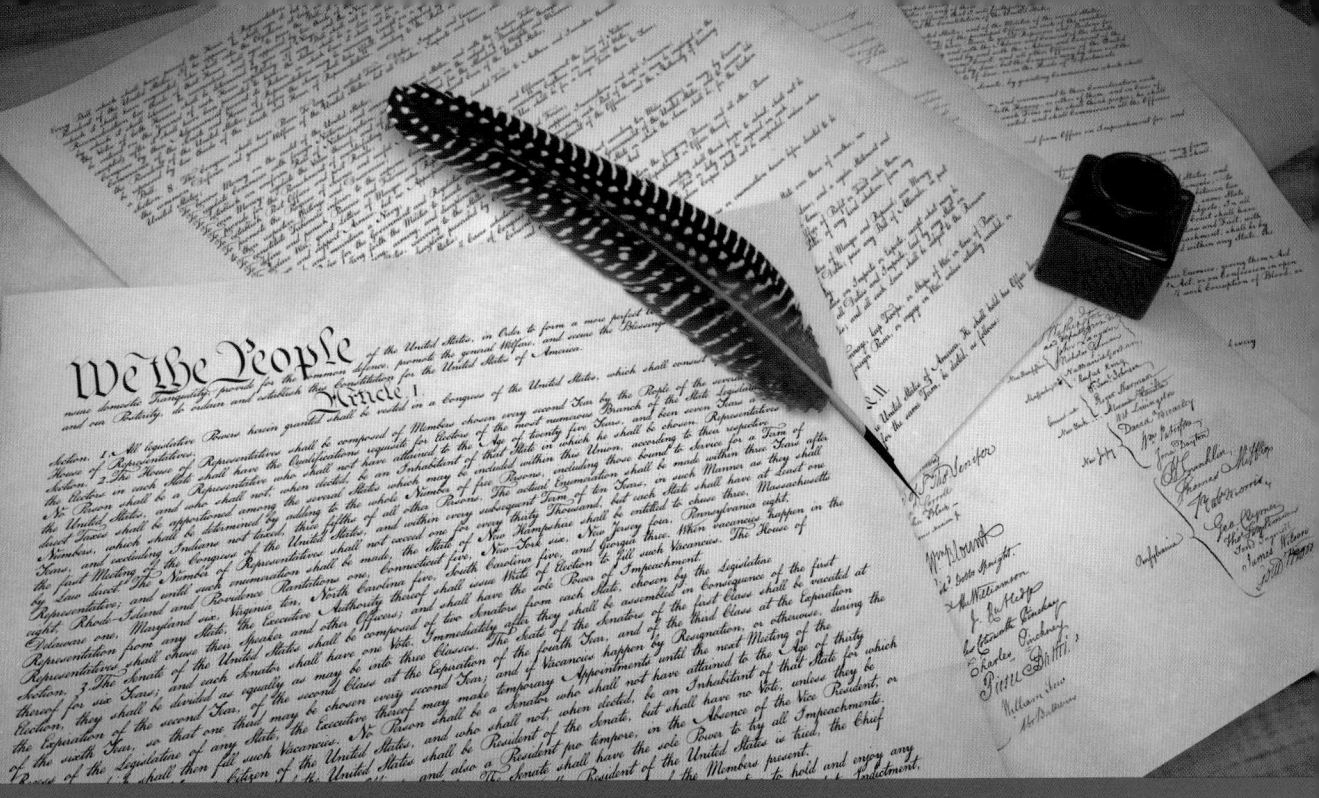

Important documents such as the U.S. Constitution were originally written out by hand.

If you aren't a science fan, there are **crowdsourcing** projects beyond science, too. Before we had typewriters, computers, or smartphones, millions of documents from North American history were written by hand in cursive. Historians and other people who study the past want to be able to find useful documents fast. This means the documents need to be "translated" from cursive writing into typed characters that can be searched and sorted on computers. Imagine how long it would take for a small team of experts to work through a million documents! Crowdsourcing is making it possible for experts to move faster than ever before. For example, the Smithsonian Institution, one of America's greatest collections of **artifacts**, is looking for volunteers to transcribe its documents. Check it out at *https://transcription.si.edu.*

Try This

Is science not your bag? There are lots of other nonscience crowdsourcing projects. For example, Wikipedia is a crowd-sourced project. Its content is written, edited, and evaluated by volunteers.

For More Information

BOOKS

Fontichiaro, Kristin. *Citizen Science*. Ann Arbor, MI: Cherry Lake Publishing, 2018.

Smolan, Rick, and Jennifer Erwitt. *The Human Face of Big Data*. Sausalito, CA: Against All Odds Productions, 2012.

WEB SITES

PBS: The Human Face of Big Data
www.pbs.org/program/human-face-big-data
Learn more about the interaction between people and Big Data in this PBS program and Web site.

Zooniverse
www.zooniverse.org
Contribute to a Big Data set about science and the natural world around you! Ask an adult before you set up an account.

GLOSSARY

algorithms (AL-guh-rih-thuhmz) math formulas that are used to process data and find patterns

analyst (AN-uh-list) someone who studies data and uses it to draw conclusions about the way something works

artifacts (AHR-tuh-fakts) objects made or changed by humans, especially tools or weapons used in the past

composite (kuhm-PAH-zit) something that is made up of many parts from different sources

crowdsourcing (CROWD-sor-sing) when many people contribute ideas or help to a project

inventory (IN-vuhn-tor-ee) a list of all the items that are on hand for sale in a store

personas (pur-SOH-nuhz) made-up people whose data represent a large group of actual people

server (SUR-vur) a computer that stores data and can be accessed by other connected computers

INDEX